D1064696

DELAWARE

JAKE RAJS

FOREWORD BY
RUSSELL W. PETERSON

PUBLISHED BY THE JARED COMPANY
WILMINGTON, DELAWARE

Page 1: Caesar Rodney statue, Wilmington

Pages 2-3: Snow geese, Bombay Hook National Wildlife Refuge, Smyrna

Page 4: Amish farmer plowing field, near Dover

Pages 6-7: Nemours Mansion and Gardens, Wilmington

Pages 10-11: Snow, Breck's Mill, Hagley Museum and Library, Wilmington

Pages 14-15: Farm, outside Odessa

Copyright 1992 Jake Rajs
The Jared Company

All rights reserved. No part of this publication may be
reproduced or transmitted in any form without the written
permission of the Jared Company, Book Division.

THE JARED COMPANY
510 Philadelphia Pike
Wilmington, DE 19809

Published in 1992
Printed in Hong Kong
Library of Congress Catalog Card Number 92-23810
ISBN: 0-89802-617-2
First Edition September 1992

PHOTOGRAPHER: Jake Rajs
PUBLISHER: Maxim Dadoun
DESIGN: Jacelen Pete
FOREWORD: Russell W. Peterson
EDITING: Andrea Tronslin

CONTENTS

To my daughter Chloe

ACKNOWLEDGMENTS

Many thanks to all the wonderful people and organizations throughout Delaware who helped with this book:

The Delaware Development Office, particularly the Windley and Allen families: Gigi, Larry and Tara Windley, and Ivy, Rico, Kyle and Rico Allen. This book would not have been possible without their professional expertise and friendship.

The Farm Home Administration, the Department of Agriculture and the many farms, the farmers and their families, and their staff members, all of whom were so cooperative: Fifer Orchards, Baker Farms, Lovett's Farm, Papen Farm, Carlisle Farm, and Laurel Farmer's Auction Market.

Chuck and Pat Wagner, Ross and Linda Collins, the Olson family, Maxim Dadoun and family (Avi and Jared). Gilda Hannah, Joe Pobereskin, Anne Rajs, Frances Rajs, Mark Speed, Jimmy Winstead, Grant Parrish, Dover Airbase, University of Delaware, Hagley Museum and Library, Nemours Museum and Gardens, Winterthur Museum and Gardens, Luther Towers, Dupont Hotel, Hampton Inn, Holiday Inn, Marriott Hotel, Sheraton Hotel, Radisson Hotel and Days Inn.

PREFACE

I embarked on the project of a visual story about Delaware because I wanted to reveal what I felt was unique about the state: the chateau country of the Brandywine in the north, the farmland in the south that resembles the American heartland, and the magnificent shoreline with one of this country's largest concentration of shorebirds. My last book, *America,* was about this entire country. I chose to focus on Delaware because I saw the opportunity to go deeper into America — the chance to get closer to the personality of this state, which my prior experiences had taught me held roots of pure America.

In over two years of driving from the rural to the industrial, I came to see Delaware as a microcosm of the United States. In as much as the United States is about diversity, for me this first state of the Union contains much of all that exists throughout the heart of this country. Farms, cities, beaches, industry, history, nature — a diversity of places and lifestyles. I have tried to be democratic, to photograph the spectrum from a teenager tumbling in the surf, to a little girl throwing stones into the Brandywine River, to the aura of the Point to Point race.

Many of the moments captured in these photographs evoke cherished memories. An especially inspiring scene occurred during a November sunset in Bombay Hook National Wildlife Refuge. I was driving down an otherwise deserted dirt road and stopped my car. Suddenly there came the honking of thousands and thousands of snow geese as they returned to the ponds for the evening. With the sky saturated with snow geese, I felt an exhilaration which the earliest Americans must also have felt while engulfed by this spectacle of nature.

The marvel of nature and the ability to return to a simpler time are among the experiences that will keep me coming back to Delaware. When close to Dover, I always try to take a certain road near Pearsons Corner. I park my car and watch the Amish drive by in buggies, farm the land, and walk down the road. Often I see children playing. Here there are no telephone poles. America: unadorned and pre-industrial.

During these few years it's been my privilege and delight to know the people of this state and explore the breadth of the landscape. I have been befriended by many open and kind people who encouraged me to feel at home. Their affection for Delaware is contagious. I hope you enjoy these photographs as much as I enjoyed taking them.

FOREWORD

Our Delaware has been appropriately called the First State, the Diamond State, the Small Wonder, the Corporation State, a Model State, and a microcosm of America. This book beautifully portrays the natural and human-made environment plus the historical and cultural sites that testify to Delaware's right to those titles. It also displays Jake Rajs's love for this little gem of a state and demonstrates once again his ability as America's premier photographer.

Since its birth, Delaware has been attracting people from all over the globe. Today, in this small state of only 2,000 square miles (0.06% of America) and with only 666,000 people in 1990 (0.26% of Americans), a sampling of many of the ethnic groups on earth lives harmoniously, a testimony to the possibility of peace on earth someday. This creative mix of humans has contributed much to the history of America, capitalized on and protected the bounteous territory they occupied, and provided exemplary leadership in science, business, government, and the arts. Although the state as a whole has prospered, there still remains, in this microcosm of America, an underprivileged portion of the community struggling in poverty, providing an important challenge for the state in the years ahead.

Two-thirds of Delaware's people live in the northernmost of its three counties, New Castle, primarily in the metropolitan area around Wilmington and Newark. Here are located the headquarters and research centers of three multinational businesses, Du Pont, Hercules, and ICI Americas; the University of Delaware; the credit card operations of many national banks; and several large industrial plants. North of Wilmington in the beautiful Chateau Country lie the estates of the large du Pont family and many wealthy business executives. A deep water canal bisects the county, providing a corridor for ocean and recreational vessels to move between Delaware and Chesapeake bays.

The lower two counties are primarily agricultural with large areas of their open, unspoiled land dedicated to wildlife refuges and parks. A prominent feature in Kent County is Dover, the state capital, with its many historical buildings and landmarks. Dover Air Force Base is home to half of the United States's huge C-5A military cargo planes that busily carry materials to every corner of the world. The Delaware State Fair at Harrington annually shows off the products and accomplishments of Delaware's prosperous agricultural business.

In Sussex County the Atlantic seashore, with its large influx of summer vacationers, is the dominant feature. So many come from Washington, D.C. that the Rehoboth Beach area is known as the "Nation's Summer Capital." Sussex County is the birthplace of two major world industries — the modern poultry industry and the nylon industry launched by Du Pont in 1939 at Seaford.

Sussex County is also the home of a few Nanticoke Indians, the only remaining descendants of the Native Americans who inhabited these flourishing hunting and fishing grounds in 1609 when the first Europeans, the English sea captain Henry Hudson and his crew, in the hire of the Dutch East Indies Company, explored Delaware Bay.

Twenty-two years later, 28 Dutch colonists, under the auspices of the Dutch West India Company, landed at Cape Henlopen and established Zwaanendael, the first European settlement in Delaware at present day Lewes. Unfortunately, within one year it was wiped out in a conflict with the natives who had discovered the area hundreds of years before.

Several colonists, unhappy with the Dutch West Indies Company, organized the New Sweden Company with the support of the Swedish government. The company set out to establish a Swedish colony in the New World led by the Dutch explorer Peter Minuit. In 1638, he and his crew of 22 Swedish and Dutch sailors founded the first permanent colony in Delaware, Fort Christina, now present day Wilmington. The Swedish government bought out the Dutch interests and over several years markedly reinforced their colony with Swedish and Finnish settlers. "The Rocks," where the Swedish expedition first landed, is now marked by a monument purchased by the schoolchildren of Sweden on the 300th anniversary of the landing.

In 1651 the Dutch governor of New Amsterdam (New York), Peter Stuyvesant, established Fort Casimir and its surrounding settlement, New Amstel, just six miles downriver from Fort Christina. After three years the Swedish colonists forced the surrender of Fort Casimir, but Peter Stuyvesant returned one year later, putting an end to Swedish authority in the area.

For the next eight years the two colonies prospered under Dutch authority but in 1664 the English, under the Duke of York, the future King James II, forced their surrender. In 1673, the Dutch recaptured and held the Delaware settlements but surrendered them again to the English the following year. The English maintained control for the next 102 years until the 13 English colonies declared their independence in 1776.

New Castle is where the Quaker leader William Penn first came ashore in 1682 to claim his lease to what became Pennsylvania, plus the "lower three counties on the Delaware." These three counties gave him so much trouble in 1701, he permitted them to have their own legislative body in New Castle. The capital remained there until 1777 when it was temporarily moved to Dover to escape the threat of the British fleet in Delaware Bay. The move was made permanent in 1781. Today New Castle proudly shows off its historic sites and the many homes that have been continuously occupied since pre-Revolutionary War times.

William Penn's heirs had trouble with the Calverts of Maryland who claimed title to Sussex County. In 1763, an English court settled the matter giving Sussex to the Penn family and assigned two surveyors, Charles Mason and Jeremiah Dixon, to mark the official border between Delaware and Maryland.

Delaware played an important role in the signing of the Declaration of Independence. Of its three delegates to the Continental Congress in Philadelphia, Caesar Rodney, and Thomas McKean were in favor of independence, and George Read was opposed. But Rodney was in Dover, ill with cancer. Since a unanimous vote of the 13 states was required, a message was sent to Rodney encouraging him to come to Philadelphia. On July 1 and 2, 1776, he rode 80 miles in rain and thunder to cast the deciding vote. Delaware celebrates its most famous son with a beautiful bronze statue in Rodney Square in Wilmington depicting the courageous Caesar Rodney on his galloping horse heading toward Philadelphia.

Of special pride to Delawareans is the unanimous vote to ratify the United States Constitution on December 7, 1787. This made Delaware the First State. To this day, its flag and its governors are given priority at ceremonial events throughout the country.

When in 1860 the leaders of the secessionist states tried to convince Delaware to join the Confederacy, they were told that the First State to join the union would be the last to leave it. Although Delaware, where slavery was legal and approved by many, stayed loyal to the Union during the Civil War, some families in southern Delaware supported and fought with the South.

Northern Delaware around Wilmington had from the early 1700s been industrializing. Using water power from the Brandywine River, mills producing such items as leather goods, flour, paper, and textiles were gradually established. Later ships, wagons, and railroad cars were manufactured in the area. Of special importance was the establishment on the Brandywine in 1802 of a black powder mill by Eleuthère Irénée du Pont, an immigrant from France, who had learned his trade under Lavoisier, the famous French chemist. E.I. du Pont de Nemours and Co. became a vital supplier of explosives for the military and for major excavation projects.

The Hagley Museum is a working restoration of du Pont's initial powder mills, workers' homes, and the owner's mansion on 230 acres along the Brandywine River. It is an inspiring depiction of the birth of an American industry. The Winterthur Museum is a legacy of Henry F. du Pont. He converted his lifelong home into a world class museum with 196 period room settings displaying over 80,000 objects of American decorative arts. Winterthur's beautiful rolling land is the home of the popular annual Point to Point Races.

In 1912 the Du Pont Company was forced by federal antitrust laws to split into three companies, Du Pont, Hercules, and Atlas. The latter two also grew into large diversified research-oriented chemical companies, and Atlas was subsequently acquired by ICI Americas. As a result Wilmington claims the title of Chemical Capital of the World.

Delaware's fertile farmland has long supported a thriving agribusiness. Today its major activity is producing corn and soybeans, much of it used as feed for the approximately 200 million chickens produced in lower Delaware annually and sold in the nation's markets.

Delaware's first-rate museums, historical sites, popular race tracks, diverse parks, wildlife refuges, and, above all, superb beaches have led to a large recreation and tourism business and contributed markedly to the quality of life in this Diamond State.

Delaware's coastal zone is a great place for fishing, boating, hunting, swimming, crabbing, surfing, hiking, bicycling, bird-watching, studying nature, or just lying in the sun. It's a magnet that attracts people throughout Delaware and its adjoining areas to enjoy its attractive, natural environment.

Much of the land in the coastal zone is held in perpetuity for the enjoyment of its natural values. One special area is Bombay Hook National Wildlife Refuge with its 16,280 acres of wetlands, woods, and impoundments. Over 300 species of birds inhabit the area. Roads on the extensive dikes and several observation towers make viewing the wildlife a pleasure. In late fall and early winter tens of thousands of snow geese and lesser numbers of Canada geese put on a spectacular show. Overhead you may see one of the bald eagles that nest on the refuge.

Each spring the wetlands along Delaware Bay provide one of America's great bird spectacles. About one million shorebirds from South America stop on the way to their Arctic breeding grounds. They feast on the eggs of horseshoe crabs before continuing their journey north.

Delaware's treasured coastal area was threatened in the late 1960s when a consortium of 13 large international oil companies planned, with the U.S. Department of Commerce and Delaware interests, to build several refineries and associated petrochemical complexes along the shore, dredge a deepwater port and create two large islands in Delaware Bay for transshipment of bulk products. Shell Oil Company was ready to start building a huge refinery on 5,000 acres which had been rezoned for that purpose. The rezoning had been upheld by the Delaware Supreme Court.

The state had to make a choice. The opportunity for extensive industrialization was incompatible with the way of life in Delaware's pristine natural areas. After two years of intense debate, the state passed the Delaware Coastal Zone Act in June 1971. This act prohibits any more heavy industry or bulk product transfer facilities in Delaware's coastal zone. This legislation earned Delaware an international reputation for preserving its environment. For over 21 years the Act has withstood repeated challenges in the legislature and in Delaware and Federal courts.

Delaware has maintained both its unspoiled coast and a booming economy, good reasons for calling it a Model State.

I have purposely laced this foreword with many facts and figures, as Delaware is a state rich in history and heritage. Now, turn the pages of this book and enjoy the romantic, often lyrical, interpretations of our state by master photographer, Jake Rajs. May the two approaches mingle in your mind to make your journey both informative and beautiful.

Russell W. Peterson

Governor of Delaware (1969-1973)
President of National Audubon Society (1979-1985)
Chairman of United States Council on Environmental Quality (1973-1976)

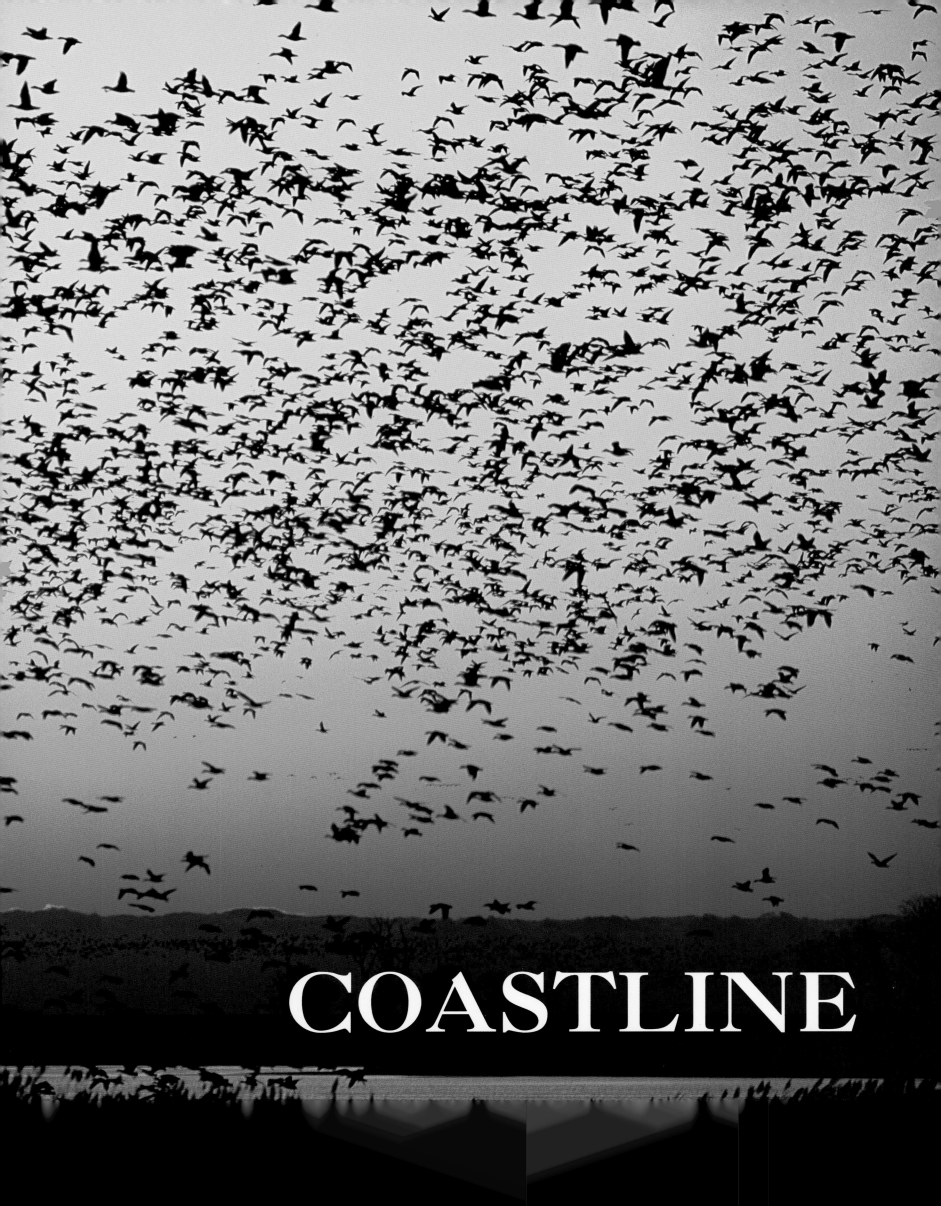

COASTLINE

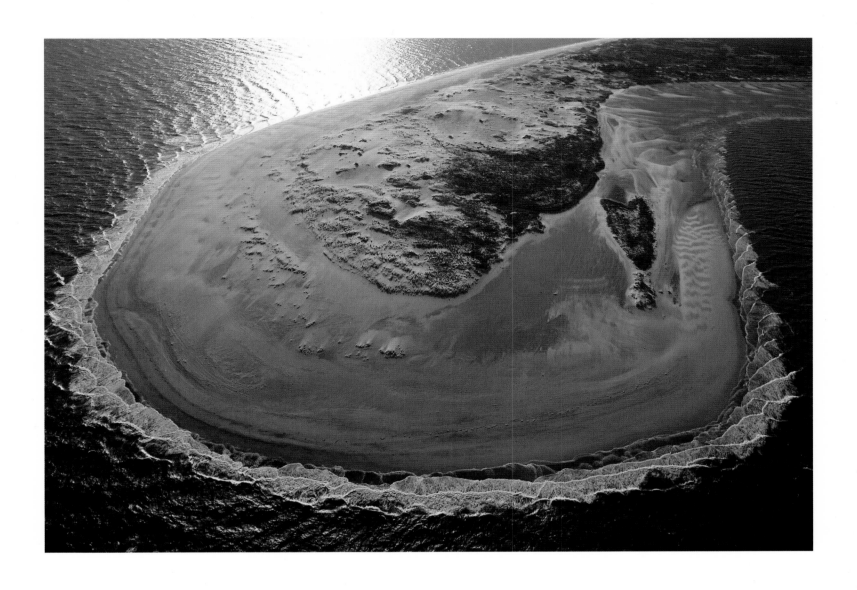

Page 39 (above): Great egret, Bombay Hook National Wildlife Refuge, Smyrna

Page 39 (below): Sandcastles, Rehoboth Beach

Pages 40-41: Inner Harbor Lighthouse, Lewes

Pages 42-43: Snow geese, Bombay Hook National Wildlife Refuge, Smyrna

Page 44: Little girl, Bethany Beach

Page 45 (above): Boats, Indian River Inlet

Page 45 (below): Fishing, Bethany Beach

Page 47 (above): East Coast Skim Board Championship, Dewey Beach

Page 47 (below): East Coast Skim Board Championship, Dewey Beach

Pages 48-49: Semipalmated sandpipers, Port Mahon

Page 50: Great blue herons, Bombay Hook National Wildlife Refuge, Smyrna

Page 51: Great egret, Bombay Hook National Wildlife Refuge, Smyrna

Pages 52-53: Mother and daughter, Bethany Beach

HEARTLAND

Pages 54-55: Amish woman, Pearsons Corner

Pages 56-57: Fishing, Lums Pond State Park, Kirkwood

Page 58 (above): Pig racing, Delaware State Fair, Harrington

Page 58 (below): Rodeo, Delaware State Fair, Harrington

Page 59: Junior Lamb Feeding Contest, Delaware State Fair, Harrington

Pages 60-61: Delaware State Fair, Harrington

59

Page 62: Return Day, Georgetown

Page 63 (above): Maypole Dancing, Old Dover Days, Dover

Page 63 (below): Old Dover Days, Dover

Pages 64-65: Hot-air Balloon Festival, Milton

Pages 66-67: Hot-air Balloon Festival, Milton

Page 68: Nanticoke Indian Powwow, Oak Orchard

Page 69: Nanticoke Indian Powwow, Oak Orchard

Pages 70-71: Bald Cypress trees, Canada geese, Trussum Pond, Laurel

Page 80: Strawberry picking, Lovett's Farm, Odessa

Page 81: Laurel Farmer's Auction, Laurel

Pages 82-83: Baling straw, Odessa

Pages 84-85: Asparagus picking, Odessa

BRANDYWINE

Page 116: Wilmington Public Library

Page 117: Grand Opera House, Wilmington